Catch
a Falling Teacher

Take Time to Breathe, Relax, and
Let Go . . .

By Dr. Connie R. Hebert
Motivational Speaker for Educators
Illustrated by Sheila Hanifin

Breathe, relax,
let go!
Connie Hebert

To order additional copies of this book, contact:
Xlibris Corporation
1-888-795-4274
www.Xlibris.com
Orders@Xlibris.com

Dedicated to my husband & best friend,
David, for catching me . . .

Introduction

We all need to breathe, relax, and let go! This special and very personal book was designed for all who teach, live, or work with children. As educators and parents, we sometimes find ourselves falling into a whirlwind of stress, boredom, fatigue, anxiety, pressure, and loneliness. In essence, we forget to utilize the power of the 'present moment.' There is little time to reflect on who we are, what we do, and why we do what we do. When we set aside time to breathe, focus, and think, we give ourselves the 'gift of energy.' This makes us better teachers and happier people.

Each page of this book offers two ways to 'catch a falling teacher.' The first is an action; the second, a reaction. Each action requires inward focus and deliberate action; each reaction requires reflection and awareness. Remember that writing is just thinking through the pen. Without the 'reaction,' the action is something that you did and that's all it is. When we write about what we discover as a result of the action, we create awareness within. Over time, this growing awareness will work to create daily energy, self-discipline, and creativity.

I invite you to use this book to lift your spirits and enrich your daily life so that you may be an 'energized teacher' every single day.

Tired Teachers vs. Energized Teachers
by Connie R. Hebert, Ed.D.

Tired teachers . . .	Energized teachers . . .
~ work hard	~ work smart
~ are hard copies	~ are originals
~ repeat things	~ develop new things
~ focus on time	~ focus on children
~ rely on support	~ rely on instincts
~ see a daily view	~ see the horizon
~ ask when and where	~ ask why and how
~ plan, plan, & plan	~ assess, reflect, & then plan
~ accept poor leadership	~ challenge weak leaders
~ are good soldiers	~ are an inspiration
~ touch lives	~ touch hearts
~ hold onto stress	~ breathe, relax, & let go

Ask yourself 2 questions:

- "What are 2 words that describe me at my best?"

- "How often am I at my best?"

What I discovered: _____
_____
_____
_____

Accept the weather, just for today, no matter what it is.

Repeat this line to yourself throughout the day: "I refuse to allow the weather to affect how I feel. . . "

What I discovered: _____

_____

_____

_____

After lunch today, close your eyes for a few moments. Now firmly squeeze the tip of each finger with the other hand, slowly.

Allow your eyes to open.

What I discovered: _____

_____

_____

_____

Breathe deeply, at least 3 times today. Remember to exhale completely.

While you breathe, let go of the need to be perfect.

What I discovered: _____
_____
_____
_____

Buy yourself a beautiful flower.

Bring it to school or put it in a special spot at home. Now, breathe deeply, in and out, as you smell your flower at least three times today.

What I discovered: _____

_____

_____

_____

Before going home today, write down 3 **new** things you taught your students today.

How did you know these were new?

What I discovered: _____

_____

_____

_____

Crinkle something up with both of your hands. You might use a newspaper page, paper bag, or sheet of foil.

Close your eyes as you slowly squeeze your fingers around it, tightly.
Now, open your eyes and let go!

What I discovered: _____

_____

_____

_____

Clap loudly for something your students do today.

Don't forget to smile while you clap!

What I discovered: _____

_____

_____

_____

Capture a few 'precious moments' in your classroom or home today.

How will you do that?

What I discovered: _____

_____

_____

_____

Decide which of the following areas could stand improvement:

Voice

Pace

Body Language

Eye Contact

Focus on this area for several weeks . . .

What I discovered: _____

_____

_____

_____

Design a 'ME' collage to share with students.

Do this by cutting and pasting together pictures that tell of your interests, hobbies, talents, dreams, and experiences.

What I discovered: _____

_____

_____

_____

Drink a **whole** cup of coffee, tea, or other beverage **without** doing anything else.

Notice how the cup or bottle feels in your hand. Tune into sensations in your throat and thoughts in your mind . . .

What I discovered: _____

_____

_____

_____

Every time you walk up or downstairs, in and out of the bathroom, or back and forth to your car, count your steps.

$$1 \ldots 2 \ldots 3$$
GO!

What I discovered: _____

_____

_____

_____

Everybody needs a 'thinking place.'

Write down 3 places where you can just sit and think. Make time to go to one of these and use it!

What I discovered: _____

_____

_____

_____

Encourage 3 people to try something in life that matches their strengths or talents. If you don't know what these are, find out!

Make a mental note of their reactions . . .

What I discovered: _____

_____

_____

_____

Feel your feet as they press into your shoes, just for today.

Notice how your toes feel when you walk, stand, sit, and drive.

What I discovered: _____

_____

_____

_____

Find some time today to tell your students **why** you became a teacher.

Ask them if they know what a 'certified' teacher is . . .

What I discovered: _____

_____

_____

_____

Figure out, on average, how long it takes for you to eat your lunch!

From now on, try **doubling** that time and take note of how you do that.

What I discovered: _____

_____

_____

_____

Give away **something** that is important to you to **someone** who is important to you.

Is it a hug, compliment, favorite thing, smile, your time, or something else?

What I discovered: _____

_____

_____

_____

Gather something today . . .

- A bunch of flowers
- A group of kids
- A bowl of berries
- A bouquet of dandelions

It doesn't matter what you gather . . . just gather!

What I discovered: _____

_____

_____

_____

Go outside and look up!

Now slowly lower your head to rest your chin on your chest while you take in a long, deep breath and let out a long, slow breath.

What I discovered: _____

_____

_____

_____

Hum a favorite tune, softly to yourself, every time you are alone today.

Notice what your mind is doing while you hum . . .

What I discovered: _____

_____

_____

_____

Help 3 people who do not ask for your help.

It is the act of helping someone, for the sole purpose of easing a burden, that matters most.

What I discovered: _____

_____

_____

_____

Have a 'chat' with yourself today!

Tell yourself 3 things you are proud of, 3 things you want to do, and 3 things that you wish someone would say to you.

What I discovered: _____

_____

_____

_____

Inspect your desk drawers!

Throw away anything you do not need.
Material clutter leads to mental clutter...

What I discovered: _____

_____

_____

_____

Improve just one procedure in your classroom today.

You may want to put tennis balls on the 'feet' of your classroom chairs or institute a "10 seconds to get here" policy for the start of small group lessons.

What I discovered: _____

_____

_____

_____

If you can find some grass today, go outside and sit in it. Search for a 4-leaf clover.

Focus only on counting clover leaves. You may actually get lucky and find one!

What I discovered: _____

_____

_____

_____

Just for today, look in the mirror and tell yourself 3 things you like about yourself.

Focus on these things all day long . . .

What I discovered: _____

_____

_____

_____

Jot down ALL the places that you would like to visit in your lifetime. Don't leave any of them out . . .

Now put a star* next to 3 places that you absolutely must see. What do you need to do to make this happen?

What I discovered: _____

_____

_____

_____

Join hands with a few children to form a circle.

Together, move towards the middle, raising your arms and looking up.
Together, move back, lowering your arms. Now, make it fun!

What I discovered: _____

_____

_____

_____

Kindness can work wonders if it is practiced on a daily basis.

Do or say something 'kind' to 3 others today. Don't wait around for a response. Just do it!

What I discovered: _____

_____

_____

_____

Knock on a door or a wall for a few minutes today!

Try making your 'knock' loud, soft, easy, hard, staggered, fun, and powerful. Notice what your mind is doing as you perform these actions . . .

What I discovered: _____

_____

_____

_____

Know when to stop pushing yourself . . .

When your body tells you to sit down, sit down. When your eyes want to close, allow them to close. When your mind starts to wander, bring it back to your breath.

What I discovered: _____

_____

_____

_____

Look into the eyes of children and then tell them why they are special.

Be sure to smile 'with your eyes' when you tell them . . .

What I discovered: _____

_____

_____

_____

Listen to music for at least 10 minutes today.

Focus on what your mind and breath are doing as you listen.

What I discovered: _____

_____

_____

_____

Lift your chin up toward the ceiling, slowly and steadily.

Now let your head simply 'fall back' as you close your eyes. Notice what is happening in your neck, forehead, and eyelids.

What I discovered: _____

_____

_____

_____

Make a list of 10 things you are grateful for.

How many of them involve money?

How many of them do you have the power to change?

How many do you actually 'own'?

What I discovered: _____

_____

_____

_____

Move gently and steadily all day long.

If you start to gather speed, deliberately slow yourself down!

Slow, gentle, focused movements . . .

What I discovered: _____

_____

_____

_____

Motivate yourself by doing something you do NOT like to do, but HAVE to do.

It might involve finishing something, cleaning something, or starting something.
Notice what your mind is 'saying' while you are doing this . . .

What I discovered: _____

_____

_____

_____

Napping is beneficial and necessary for inner peace.

Make time to close your eyes just long enough to 'fall' into a nap. Do this every day for at least 1 month, taking note of how you feel each day.

What I discovered: _____

_____

_____

_____

Navigate your way through the day, as if you were a captain of a ship.

Have a plan, but respond to each issue and challenge **only** when it occurs. Notice your ability to be flexible at times and adaptable at others . . .

What I discovered: _____

_____

_____

_____

Notice what your neck and shoulders are doing, all day long!

As you observe these 2 areas, make slight adjustments to release tension and stress.

What I discovered: _____

_____

_____

_____

Organize something today!

It may be a drawer, desk, closet, or purse.
It doesn't matter what it is. Just make time to do it.

What I discovered: _____

_____

_____

_____

Orchestrate a plan for an upcoming weekend, as if you were writing a symphony.

Include something fast and fun, something slow and relaxing, something loud and energizing, and then . . . a big finish!!

What I discovered: _____

_____

_____

_____

Open your mind today . . .

Ask someone a question about something that you know absolutely nothing about.

What I discovered: _____

_____

_____

_____

Prepare a list, first thing in the morning, of every single thing you are going to eat and drink, just for today.

Check off each item throughout the day.

What I discovered: _____

_____

_____

_____

Pick out an object and stare at it.

Mentally, take note of 'picky' little details about the object. Notice what your mind is doing as you practice this powerful activity.

What I discovered: _____

_____

_____

_____

Pretend you are a child who is watching you teach!

Now ask yourself the following:
- What do I hear?
- What do I see around me?
- What does the pace suggest to me?
- How am I feeling about myself?
- Where would I like to be?

What I discovered: _____

_____

_____

_____

Quit talking so much!!

Let the kids and others talk **way** more than you do. Just for today!

What I discovered: _____

_____

_____

_____

Quack at kids instead of using words!

See if they can guess what you mean . . .
"Quack, quack." = "Sit down."
"Quack, quack, quack, quack?" = "Where is your
  pencil?"
"Quack, quack, quack." = "Raise your hand."

What I discovered: _____

_____

_____

_____

Question anyone who makes you doubt yourself this week . . .

You might ask the following:
- "What do you mean?"
- "Why do you think so?"
- "Can you tell me why you think that?"
- "Do you really think so?"

What I discovered: _____

_____

_____

_____

Respond to someone just with your eyes.

See how many ways you can send a message without saying a word!

What I discovered: _____

_____

_____

_____

Recite a nursery rhyme, short poem, or simple phrase over and over again, for just a few minutes today.

Notice what your mind is focusing on as you do this.

What I discovered: _____

_____

_____

_____

Renew your spirit.

Take a walk outside, no matter what the weather is. If you find your mind wandering away from the present moment, recite the following:

"Right here, right now."

What I discovered: _____

_____

_____

_____

Sit as still as you can with your eyes open or shut.

Do this for at least 10 minutes today.
No wiggling allowed!

What I discovered: _____

_____

_____

_____

Simplify this day by focusing **only** on what you see, what you feel, and what you hear, at any given moment of time.

Can your recall any details of that moment?

What I discovered: _____

_____

_____

_____

Sing a favorite tune over and over again throughout the day.

Can you hum it, whistle it, or 'sing' it silently? Notice what you mind is doing and not doing.

What I discovered: _____

_____

_____

_____

Tell yourself what your greatest strength is. The opposite of this is your greatest weakness.

Now focus on these all day long.

What I discovered: _____

_____

_____

_____

Try something new for 3 days in a row.

It may be a new food, new drink, new shampoo, or new radio station. It doesn't matter what it is as long as it is new!

What I discovered: _____

_____

_____

_____

Talk softly and gently to every person you meet all day long today.

Catch yourself if you find your voice 'louder than soft.' How will you do that?

What I discovered: _____

_____

_____

_____

Understand how someone else feels about something.

To do this, you may have to ask open ended questions while 'using your eyes' to listen.

What I discovered: _____

_____

_____

_____

Undo something that is simply not working.

It may be the way you begin or end your lessons, collect papers, or leave your desk at the end of the day . . .

Whatever it is, undo it and redo it!

What I discovered: _____
_____
_____
_____

Upgrade yourself to a new and better chair!

Go on a mission to replace a chair in your life that does not offer comfort and peaceful rest.

What I discovered: _____

_____

_____

_____

Value your work with kids . . .

Share a technique or a teaching method with someone who is younger than you are.

What I discovered: _____

_____

_____

_____

Vary the way in which you start each day.

For one whole week, try drinking your coffee before you get dressed, playing music while you get ready, buying a new alarm clock with a different ringer, or taking a different route to work.

What I discovered: _____

_____

_____

_____

Venture outside today with pen and paper in hand.

Jot down 3 colors you see, 3 things you hear, and 3 feelings you have while you are out there . . .

What I discovered: _____

_____

_____

_____

Wink at someone today!

Notice their reaction and try it again tomorrow with someone else. Winking is powerful!

What I discovered: _____

_____

_____

_____

Write down the names of 3 places where you can just 'play'. If you do not have any, search for them during the next month.

Then, go to one of them after work and use it!

What I discovered: _____

_____

_____

_____

Walk faster than you normally do, wherever you go today.

If you find yourself slipping back into your 'normal' speed, move it! Take note of how you feel at the end of the day.

What I discovered: _____

_____

_____

_____

Xplore a book that you have never touched before.

Teach a child how to do this . . .

What I discovered: _____

_____

_____

_____

Xplain something to yourself over and over again.

Notice whether this helps to understand it better . . . or not.

What I discovered: _____

_____

_____

_____

Xercise your mind by memorizing something today. It might be your social security number, a poem to share, or a joke to tell.

Now, tell 3 people what it is. See if you remember it one week from now.

What I discovered: _____

_____

_____

_____

Yoyo yourself, up and down in a chair, at least 10 times!

Now sit down, close your eyes, and focus on the energy that has just been released from this simple activity.

What I discovered: _____

_____

_____

_____

Yell at something inanimate . . .

It might be your car, answering machine, computer, or vacuum cleaner! Whatever it is, just 'let go' of any frustration you might be carrying.

What I discovered: _____

_____

_____

_____

Yak about something that happened to you that was incredibly funny.

See if you can make yourself, and the other person, laugh about it!

What I discovered: _____

_____

_____

_____

Zoo out, for just a few moments, in your car.

Before you start the engine, sit back, close your eyes, and notice your breathing. See if you can bring it to a slow, steady, and peaceful pace.

What I discovered: _____

_____

_____

_____

Zip a coat, jacket, or sweater all the way up and all the way down 5 times, without stopping . . .

Notice what your mind is focusing on. Now try it 10 times and see what happens.

What I discovered: _____

_____

_____

_____

Zap yourself, in your mind, to the most beautiful place you can think of.

Write down 10 things you remember about it and share this beautiful list with your students . . .

What I discovered: _____

_____

_____

_____

Teach simply,
so that you may simply,
teach.

Connie Romell Hebert
A Teacher